Hannah Lavery

Lament for Sheku Bayoh

Salamander Street

PLAYS

First published in 2021 by Salamander Street Ltd.
(info@salamanderstreet.com)

Lament for Sheku Bayoh © Hannah Lavery, 2021

ISBN: 9781914228230

10 9 8 7 6 5 4 3 2 1

'He wasn't himself the way he was acting, but then no duty of care was given to him...because he was a Black man. That's how we feel.' – Kadi Johnson

Foreword

Lament for Sheku Bayoh is a keening for a man who has been much maligned. It is also a provocation written in response to the lack of awareness to the family's long campaign for answers.

I wanted to write a lament informed by what could I discover with no special access, what could anyone find out – if they chose too. The lament comes out of all that research and all those silences too – all that turning away.

I was deeply affected by the testimony of his family and his friends, and how that contrasted with the racial stereotypes and tropes that were used to describe Sheku Bayoh. I wanted to honour the campaign's effort – all that love – their insistence that Sheku Bayoh was due more, with a lament which attempts to give a public space and demand dignity for their grief and anger. It is in the tradition of keeners, a demonstration and call for solidarity.

I wrote the Lament in 2019 and maybe now, more people know about Sheku Bayoh and understand better what the racist tropes used to describe him mean, but we're not the country we promote to others and more importantly to ourselves. People in Scotland who experience racism have to spend so much time getting people to admit racism actually exists – it is exhausting. The provocation within this play is a challenge to that devastating lie we tell ourselves – *There's nae problem here.* There is and we all deserve better, Sheku Bayoh deserved better.

Hannah Lavery, Writer & Director, July 2021

Lament for Sheku Bayoh was first performed as a work-in-progress at the Royal Lyceum Theatre Edinburgh on 5–7 August 2019, as part of Edinburgh International Festival's *You Are Here* programme.

Writer Hannah Lavery
Director/Dramaturg David Greig
Performers Saskia Ashdown, Patricia Panther and Courtney Stoddart

An online performance of the play was performed at the 2020 Edinburgh International Festival on 25–31 August, during the Covid-19 pandemic. It was co-produced by Edinburgh International Festival, National Theatre of Scotland and Royal Lyceum Theatre Edinburgh.

Writer and Director Hannah Lavery
Designer Kirsty Currie
Composer and Musician Beldina Odenyo
Movement Director Nat McCleary

Performers Saskia Ashdown, Patricia Panther and Courtney Stoddart

The production returned with in-person live audiences for the 2021 Edinburgh International Festival on 25–28 August.

Characters

FIRST KEENER

SECOND KEENER

THIRD KEENER

SINGER/FOURTH KEENER

The Lament (Part One)

SECOND: We walk our preserved battlefields. Laying stone
on towering cairns. Kilted and tearful in school assemblies
we sing of our beautiful defeats, our fallen. Ignoring anything
anyone
   who may dispute the telling.

Do we have to be on the right side
of every story we tell of ourselves –
is that belonging?

What would it cost us
to lift him broken from a Kirkcaldy street
to cradle him as our own?

Can we still say
we love this place
if we don't.

Can we still sell
this vision of ourselves
to ourselves?

Who are we
if we turn toward this?

Who are we
if we don't?

Can we have
no more of this
love wi out question?

Can we no
now
stop
looking over that border

into all that green saying
Here.
Aye
Here.

We are so
so much better.

No problem here pal.
None.
None at all.

Is it no time
after all?

Ach!

Did you know? Colour blind
they say
is a peculiar
Scottish phrase.

Pure of intention.
Pure as the driven

it's blinding.

Well until
it's not
until
you're not.

CONVERSATION ONE

FIRST: Sheku Bayoh?

THIRD: Sorry – Sheku who?

FIRST: He was –

THIRD: – Kirkcaldy? What did he do?

FIRST: Och! He was –

THIRD: – Well then. Christ, they have a hard job.

FIRST: But that's –

THIRD: – Well, there you go then.

FIRST: What?

THIRD: Dangerous times.

FIRST: For who?

THIRD: What?

FIRST: I said, for who?

FIRST PAUSE

FIRST: *(playing reporter from Fife Courier)*

On May 3, 2015, Sheku Bayoh, a thirty-one-year-old trainee gas engineer had been watching a boxing match with a friend. Police received reports of a man wielding a machete and behaving erratically at Hayfield Road, Kirkcaldy.

Police say they found Sheku and tried to engage him. He was then restrained with batons and CS spray. It is said that anywhere between six and nine officers were involved, using leg and ankle restraints. It is said that no knife was found in his possession.

Sheku's family say up to six of the nine of the officers were on top of him. He lost consciousness and never recovered.

The shock of Sheku's death in police custody was felt far and wide. Sheku's well-attended funeral was held on Sunday June 7 as mourners still waited for answers on just what had happened.

Lament (Part Two)

The Three are playing the BBC unless otherwise indicated.

FIRST: The BBC understands Mr Bayoh had taken the drug ecstasy.

SECOND: The CCTV shows Mr Bayoh approaching the police at about 07:20am.

THIRD: The BBC understands the pictures show he did not have a knife.

SECOND: *(this is second)*
Two of the nine officers? Or was it nine? Maybe it was eight, or was it four?

FIRST: *(this is First)*
Two of the officers believed they could be facing a terrorist incident. Is that understood, do we have you so far?

SECOND: A leading authority on police restraint and use of force, Eric Baskind, of Liverpool John Moore University says –

FIRST: *(playing Eric Baskind)*
What strikes me from the evidence of the officers is that they approach the scene with the intention of using force. He's not running away, he's not, at that moment in time, creating a danger to anyone. They get there, they screech to a halt, they get out of the cars with irritant sprays and batons. That to me doesn't seem measured. That is not best practice. And all of those actions were very escalatory.

SECOND: The BBC understands at least four and up to six officers were immediately involved in the encounter. That CS spray and police batons were used and within about thirty seconds Mr Bayoh was brought to the ground, face down. Handcuffs and leg restraints were applied.

THIRD: The BBC understands PC Paton and a colleague known as officer B – who were two of the first on the scene – had a combined weight of about 43 stones.

FIRST: Eyewitnesses understand that the officers were kneeling and lying on Mr Bayoh in order to restrain him.

SECOND: A civilian witness told investigators, officers were lying across Mr Bayoh for several minutes.

FIRST: *(playing civilian witness)*
I heard him screaming. It sent chills through me. I heard the man shout to get the police off him. They never moved.

SECOND: An internal police document written less than an hour after Bayoh's death said that police attended reports of a male with a machete in the street.

THIRD: *(playing police officer)*
Move along folks. Come on now. You've homes to go to.

FIRST: The BBC understands that in less than five minutes after the encounter began, Mr Bayoh was noticed to be unconscious and one officer radioed for an ambulance.

SECOND: Officer B, who is 6ft 4in and weighed 25 stone, told investigators he had Mr Bayoh pinned to the ground for –

THIRD: – a maximum of 30 seconds.

SECOND: Another said the restraint had been –

THIRD: *(playing Police Officer)*
appropriate, textbook stuff, in line with their training.

SECOND: *(playing Civilian Witness)*
I heard him screaming. It sent chills through me. I heard the man shout to get the police off him. They never moved.

FIRST: CPR was attempted by the officers, but Mr Bayoh arrived by ambulance at the town's Victoria Hospital – where his sister works – unresponsive. He was pronounced dead at 09:04.

THIRD: *(this is third)*
Okay?

SECOND: *(this is second)*
Yes.

FIRST: *(this is first)*
You all know this.

THIRD: We know all this but their Lawyer Aamer Anwar told us –

SECOND: *(playing Aamer)*

He wasn't 6ft plus, he was 5ft 10in. He wasn't super-sized, he was 12 stone 10 pounds. He wasn't brandishing a knife at a police officer. He didn't stab a police officer. In fact he wasn't carrying a knife when the police officers attended.

THIRD: *(this is third)*

It's all very complicated.

SECOND: *(this is second)*

We are told we don't understand.

THIRD: *(playing PC Short)*

Mr Bayoh's muscles were bulging and he looked aggressive.
He was not listening to commands and looked very intimidating, said PC Short.

SECOND: The BBC understands the pictures show that he did not have a knife. The Eyewitnesses understand that the officers were kneeling and lying on Mr Bayoh in order to restrain him.

FIRST: Two officers believed they could be facing a terrorist incident.

SECOND: *(this is Second)*

We understand.

THIRD: *(playing Aamer)*

He didn't attempt to stab anyone, and he wasn't found with a knife on him. Those are the actual facts.

SECOND: *(this is second)*

We are told we don't understand.

THIRD: *(PC Short)*

I have never seen anything like it before, he was like a zombie.
PC Short

SECOND: *(this is second)*

Officer?

THIRD: *(PC Short)*

I was terrified that he was going to kill a member of the public if he was allowed to leave the street, which is what he was trying to do. PC Short.

FIRST: She said her colleague used a spray on Mr Bayoh and it hit him in the face.

THIRD: *(PC Short)*

But he kept laughing and just wiped it as if it was water and kept walking in the same direction. Nothing was working and we were not in control of the situation at all. PC Short.

FIRST: She took her baton from its holster and told him to get on his knees.

Pause.

FIRST: The BBC understands PC Paton and a colleague known as officer B, who were two of the first on the scene, were understood to have a combined weight of about 43 stones.

SECOND: *(this is second)*

In driven snow. We leave –

THIRD: *(PC Short)*

Mr Bayoh appeared to be on a mission from the manner in which he was walking. He appeared out of control and dangerous and given the reports of him chasing people with a knife as well as his demeanour and the way he didn't react to the sprays, I felt that he could not be permitted to leave, I was terrified that he was going to kill a member of the public if he was allowed to leave the street, which is what he was trying to do. PC Short.

SECOND: Officer?

THIRD: *(PC Short)*

Mr Bayoh's muscles were bulging and he looked aggressive. He was not listening to commands and looked very intimidating. PC Short.

SECOND: *(this is second)*

Officer?

THIRD: *(PC Short)*

He appeared out of control and dangerous. PC Short.

SECOND: Officer?

THIRD: *(this is second)*

I have never seen anything like it before, he was like a zombie. PC Short.

SECOND: *(this is second)*

Officer, can you help?

FIRST: Following Sheku's death, PC Paton's brother-in-law Barry Swan claimed the officer was a racist. Swan claimed the officer once said: 'I'm a total racist – I hate all blacks'. Paton has denied the claims.

SECOND: *(this is second)*

You're fucking blind to it.

FIRST: Barry Swan, forty-three, said: 'He out and out admitted that he was a racist, that he hates them, as he puts it – all the blacks. It's not right he's a police officer.'

SECOND: *(this is second)*

Understand this.

THIRD: *(PC Short)*

Mr Bayoh's muscles were bulging and he looked aggressive. He was not listening to commands and looked very intimidating.

FIRST: *(this is first)*

Understand this.

SECOND: Collette Bell, Mr Bayoh's partner and the mother of his eight-month-old son Isaac, said: "They're supposed to be trained in restraint. They should have the knowledge and ability to deal with those people appropriately without having to beat them to a pulp. There are ways and means to restrain somebody without killing them.

There's no doubt about it, if Shek had not come into contact with the police he would still be here, and that hurts a lot."

FIRST: Days after his death, the Scottish Police Federation lawyer Peter Watson told the media that "a petite female police officer was subjected to a violent and unprovoked attack by a very large man who punched, kicked and stamped on her."

THIRD: *(Police Officer)*
Move along.

SECOND: *(this is second)*
Move along.

FIRST: *(Police Officer)*
Move along.

SECOND: *(Playing Civilian)*
I heard him screaming. It sent chills through me. I heard the man shout to get the police off him. They never moved.

FIRST: *(Police Officer)*
Move along.

THIRD: *(Playing Civilian)*
I heard the man shout to get the police off him. They never moved.

SECOND: *(this is second)*
Move along.

Lament (Part Three)

FIRST: Broken bones.

SECOND: Deep gash across forehead.

THIRD: Tiny blood spots in eyes.

FIRST: Injury over body.

SECOND: Face.

FIRST: Head.

SECOND: Signs of suffocation.

(Pause – Break)

THIRD: Broken bones – in broken system –

FIRST: – make safe space –

SECOND: – make that ol cage – made of rope.

THIRD: Rope of twisted threads-twisted.

FIRST: Twisting thread. Twisting of truth bound wi – we work to make rope.

SECOND: Hold the line for the good drying day.

THIRD: Hanging out to dry. Turning. Blowing in.

FIRST: Blow in.

SECOND: Blow in. Wind ye neck in pal.

FIRST: It's a good drying day. Get the rope out.

SECOND: Hang it all out to dry. The white wash – on twisting truth. Twisted fibres make rope –

THIRD: noose –

(Pause – Break.)

FIRST: – to hang.

SECOND: Let's just hang here. *(Pause.)* Till they're dried out. Till they're tired out.

THIRD: Tired. Dried out – twisting.

FIRST: Twisted. Making space. Made out of broken bone. Dark memory heart. Beating that old drum to bring them out wi white wash. Hang it out – it's a good day for drying. But the sun is too bright. It shows the marks. Burns through the magnifying glass – that wi have to look out for what is crawling beneath – the rocks we're gathering for him. Gathered by those that marched for him. Stood for two minutes in silence for him. The light through magnification creates a fire to burn – to set a light and we cannae bring in the wash now. It's full of smoke. The neighbours have been burning and we're all choking. Blind to it. Until you're not.

THIRD: Aye.

(Pause – Break.)

ALL: Until we're not.

CONVERSATION TWO

SECOND: I am in George square. There is a group of kids sitting down wi banners. *Save Our Planet* and *Protect Our Home*. They're laughing and folk are sitting on benches – watching them – ignoring them, I suppose. There are these four horses – wi four policeman – quietly standing on the other side of the Square. I don't know what to make of that... They're surely not there for the kids? A man, Asian. Walks up to the horse and strokes his head. I hold my breath. The policeman smiles. Exhale... They talk. He continues to stroke the horse's head. The man is joined by his wife (I assume) she has a baby in a buggy. They are all laughing and chatting, to these four policeman on their horses, and the protest goes on like a school picnic –

FIRST: – and what?

SECOND: I don't know. It struck me that's all. We want them to be the best of us.

FIRST: The police? Aye, suppose we do.

FIRST: But –

SECOND: – and our sympathy therefore will lie with –

FIRST: – Yes, the sympathy. It is all about where the sympathy lies. Where does it go – who is it for?

SECOND: And we share smiles with the man on the horse because he's the best of us.

FIRST: And we're suspicious of all those who try to say different –

SECOND: No smoke without fire and all that.

FIRST: Aye, no matter the truth. What the truth is – it is where our sympathy lies.

SECOND: That is the thing isn't it – where does your sympathy go?

FIRST: Where does it go? Who do we owe it to?

Lament (Part Four)

FIRST: *(Playing Fife Courier with notebook)*
The police involved were left alone, immediately after the incident, for eight hours together in the police canteen. They were given thirty-two days to make any formal statements. They had one lawyer representing them.

SECOND: Was it? Was it like this?

THIRD: Poison sipped in the police canteen – for eight hours – the nine drank from the same urn. Truth brewing to dust in their mouths. A dog whistle blown to bring the paddy vans to circle. Poison seeping out – sliding past the brass – button holing – shaping the story for thirty-two days. Lies leaking out and staining the front pages. Knocking insistent – hack – ratta tat tat – on the closed front door – knocking at the window wi its blinds pulled down in mourning. Pulling at the pain to shed more blood to be washed from their front step. Och what do I know? What do I know? *(Pause.)* And this not a new story – it's an old one. We would do well to hear it this time. No? Is it no time after all?

SECOND: Let's frame it this way – in all that low thunder coming at us from darkening skies – from those front pages – and so was it? Was it?

THIRD: High alert. High speed. CS Spray. Pumped up – at the ready. C'mon Lads – down the … *(Pause.)*

FIRST: You fall a ton – on spine – rib cracking police men.

(Pause.)

SECOND: And you don't know, what it cost us?

(Pause – Break)

THIRD: This policemen's ball – these polis shenanigans. High Alert! High speed bringing us within inches. Thirty seconds.

SECOND: You were dirt. Dust to sweep away to corners. Twenty-nine seconds.

FIRST: Put it back in that year – aye – and this year. Dog whistle… Can you hear that coming at us from the front pages – the facebook feed – the podium-the top brass? Fuel to the … Twenty seconds.

THIRD: Let's see it. Name the monster. Pull it out from under the bed. Pulled out to a Kirkcaldy street – it was to be expected – we had feared it – wanted it – high on the expectation of …

(Pause.)

Lights flashing – on high alert. High speed. Breaking – within inches *(Pause.)*
Down the…

(Pause.)

Sixteen seconds

FIRST: CS Spray at the ready. Fully pumped. Release and … Ten seconds

SECOND: Blood pumped. Pumping fully. Knee on spine. Rib cracking, some craic, polis man, down the … Eight seconds. Beast! Down the beast! C'mon Lads! The high passed down with the Polis badge. It's what uniforms are there for … Six seconds

THIRD: You don't understand – You don't know what it cost us? … Five seconds… Do you? Rib crack – break it!

(Pause – Break.)

(playing PC Short) And we did – we did your bidding. *(switches to Third)* Zero. *(switches back to PC Short)* How can you say it is all my fault?

FIRST: And are we to drown in your tears? Walk you broken – out of the courtroom – out of uniform. Thank you for your service.

SECOND: Let you out to pasture. Let you reframe it. Retell it your way?

FIRST: The nine high speed. Cs Spray at the ready. Pumped up. C'mon lads. Bring him down…
Spine kneel. Rib crack. Bring him down – *(pause.)* – polis shenanigans.

SECOND: Och! What do we know? Ach! What do we know?

SECOND PAUSE

FIRST: *(Fife Courier Reporter)*

The Police Investigations Review Commissioner is investigating. Mr Mulholland QC called for the Commissioner and the Crown Office to be allowed to 'get on with their job' amid intense media interest in the case. The intervention followed a public row between Aamer Anwar, the lawyer representing Mr Bayoh's family, and former justice secretary Kenny MacAskill. Mr Mulholland said both the Commissioner and the Crown were 'well aware of all the evidence, the lines of inquiry and the issues surrounding this case'.

THIRD: Christ!

FIRST: *(Fife Courier Reporter)*

He said: 'The Crown and the Commissioner are not influenced by the comments made in the media and that is how it should be.' However, speculation and a running commentary on the investigation can be upsetting to the family of Sheku Bayoh as well as the families of the officers involved. 'A decision will be taken at the end of this extremely complex investigation as to whether or not criminal proceedings should be raised.' Earlier this week, Mr MacAskill accused campaigners and commentators of declaring an 'open season of hunting Police Scotland' and creating a 'poisonous atmosphere' in which individual officers had been targeted.

THIRD: *(she breaks – she is devastated. It's all fucking futile.)*

....Fuck!

The Photograph (Part One)

Picture of Sheku in a kilt appears.

SECOND: Och! There he is – in his kilt.

There is a joyful bulk to him – don't you think?

The sun is shining – in that Scottish sunshine way.

Where is this then?

Is there lots of noise around you?

A wedding perhaps?

Ah! You're a captured happiness.

That big smile.

There is something of belonging here, a comfortable thing.

You're a Saturday night. A stag or better a woolf wi your pack.
You look … Och!

Maybe you have found your people.

That big ol smile, it's a winner, you charmer.

(Pause.)

Did you know?

Did you?

That one day this photie would be used to say that once you belonged
here – and that your blackness would be striking – would challenge
something…

Och!

Look!

There he is in his kilt.

CONVERSATION THREE

FIRST: And you know these guys they run toward danger while others run the other way but –

SECOND: – but what?

FIRST: What if they are the danger?

SECOND: The police? C'mon…

FIRST: Why do you say that?

SECOND: Because if it was true I would know. We would hear about it.

FIRST: Really?

SECOND: Of course, it's no Black Lives Matter and that, this is Scotland not –

FIRST: – Aye. You don't hear much about this here.

SECOND: Aye. So seriously you can't say this is anything but I don't know, a one off, a bad egg, a rotten apple.

FIRST: Aye. *(Aside.)* Rotten to its fucking core.

SECOND: Sorry?

FIRST: Nothing. It's nothing.

SECOND: No. It's obviously not. Say it.

FIRST: Say it? Say that this country – this country you love, that this country I love, my friend, is a racist one – say that?

SECOND: Not me. Not all of us, not most of us.

FIRST: Christ! What kind of response is that?

SECOND: I am not a racist.

FIRST: I'm Scottish too?

SECOND: Of course, of course you are. I never said that you –

FIRST: Then this is not an attack on you – is it? And if you say you don't see it – why not let me show you?

SECOND: Aye. Go on then but you can't say this place is racist, you can't say that?

FIRST: Why can't I?

SECOND: What's your proof?

FIRST: I have it, but you give me proof too.

SECOND: Oh! Come on.

FIRST: Okay, no, you asked. I will lay it out for you pal but you should know it's not my job to be your teacher?

SECOND: For fuck's sake you're getting too –

FIRST: Right, you want me to deliver this without emotion. You know, you ask too much of me.

SECOND: It's just, you're describing a place I don't recognise. I find it hard to believe what you say, I just –

FIRST: – You know when you say you don't believe me –

SECOND: Oh c'mon, what you say hurts me too –

FIRST: And for that you want me to apologise? So this is what I know and you know pal? You can Google as well as me – *(Googles on phone)* Okay – right – *4807 racist incidents recorded by the police in 2013–14.*

SECOND: Aye right, so where did you read that then – what's the source?

FIRST: *(Still looking on her phone.)* And this was from – The University of Glasgow – *Scotland has more of a problem with racial discrimination than some UK data would have us believe.*

SECOND: I don't know what…What I am supposed to feel?

FIRST: *(Still looking on her phone)* Here! – from The Herald – *Earlier this year, a major report on the lack of teachers from black and ethnic minority backgrounds – highlighted shocking incidents of casual racism in schools.*

SECOND: What am I to –

FIRST: *(Still looking on her phone.)* – This from the Daily Record! *Racist murders are more common in Scotland than in the rest of the UK…*

SECOND: I…I don't know what –

FIRST: It's not my problem. It's yours. It's your problem.

SECOND: My problem?

FIRST: And this dream –

SECOND: – dream?

FIRST: The dream of us that we are pushing-the rhetoric, Scotland is this place of tolerance, right? Don't you think I want that too? Don't you think I want it as much, if not more, if not more, but this – this is your problem.

SECOND: My problem?… You mean because I am white?

(Pause.)

FIRST: Aye.

SECOND: That's not fair.

FIRST: No it's not, it's not fair, but there it is.

SECOND: So what should I do then?

FIRST: You could start by listening.

SECOND: I am listening! It's just I don't –

FIRST: Don't what? You can start by seeing we have a problem, that the problem is here pal.

SECOND: So say I do that, then what?

FIRST: Then, then we start from where we really are –

SECOND: Start what?

FIRST: I don't know. I can't do all the work can I? That's not what you expect, is it?

SECOND: Christ! Listen if you hate us so much –

FIRST: Go back?

SECOND: No! I didn't say that, Jesus!

FIRST: And us? What is us? Scottish? What is that to you? Interchangeable with white? I am us too, don't you see? I'm Scottish too. I am Scotland too.

Lament (Part Five)

THIRD: The black cab driver says racist things.
  The kids on the street are saying racist things.
  The men on the train say racist things.
  My son's teacher says racist things.
  My colleagues say racist things.
  My neighbours are saying racist things.
  My newsfeed is saying racist things.
  My radio is saying racist things.
  My television is saying racist things.
  My newspaper is saying racist things.
  My politicians are saying racist things.
  My prime minister is saying racist things.
  My police are saying racist things.
  My friends are saying racist things.
  My family are saying racist things.
  My lover is saying racist things.

FIRST: I am tired.
  I am waking up
  in harr days. The fog so thick –
  it slips under the mat – under my door – into my home.
  Comes to me at the bathroom mirror – where I stand looking
  for myself
  and seeing nothing of myself there. I walk out
  of my home,
  increasingly at odds with myself here.

SECOND: In the dreich. I am head down.
  I walk hurriedly, deftly.
  I avoid the familiar pitfalls and go headlong into new walls –
  into recently dug ditches and trench. Fall
  into new cracks – opened up by your heavy boot.

THIRD: I am stripped to the bone –

in all your acid words –
in all your acid looks.
I am tired.

THIRD PAUSE

FIRST: *(BBC Reporter)*
BBC News April 2019

Two police officers involved in the Sheku Bayoh case are to be allowed to retire on medical grounds. The Scottish Police Authority was told to reconsider its decision to block the move until it was known if the officers would face criminal charges.

Now it has been revealed PC Alan Paton and PC Nicole Short, who took their case to the Court of Session in Edinburgh, will be able to step down. Both have been on long-term sick leave since Mr Bayoh's death and had asked to retire.

Lord Woolman ruled the reasons for blocking the officers' retirement 'do not add up'.

The Scottish Police Federation, which represents the two officers, welcomed the fresh decision.

It said it made clear 'these officers suffered significant injury in the execution of their duties and qualify to retire on grounds of ill-health'.

The solicitor acting on behalf of Mr Bayoh's family and partner criticised the decision which 'ultimately means that these officers cannot be subject to potential misconduct hearings or disciplinary action'.

Lawyer Aamer Anwar added: "In four years the family have been told to keep quiet so as not to prejudice a potential prosecution whilst Sheku has been subjected to smears, lies and racial stereotypes. The dead cannot answer back, but Sheku's family will, for him

THIRD: *(devastated)*
Stripped to the bone.
(Pause.)
I am tired.

Lament (Part Six)

FIRST: My beautiful brown boy. Welcome to your world. My love. Oh my sweet child, let me teach you your words. Hold your tongue. Hold your hand as you cross the road – as you leap pass the cracks. Don't fall in.

(Pause.)

Don't fall for it son. Let me hold you – until you fall asleep in my arms. Let me… Let you dream.

Dream, my boy, I'll fight the demons – the nightmares gathering in black shirts – in combat boots – in high vis vests – in hipster yellow t-shirts – wrapped in flags – in suits and in brass button uniform. Let me give you night light and night light and night light to comfort you in the darkness. To light your way home. Teach you the secret histories of you and I that sit in the underground vaults and let me knit those stories to bullet proof vest for you.

My beautiful son.

My beautiful brown boy. Welcome to your world. Let me tell you that the monsters are not under your bed, are not confined to the pages of fairy tales. Let me show you where they are, who they are, teach you their secret codes, let me show you how to avoid them, to pacify them, let me teach you to eat the injustice, to swallow it and to later spit it up into your Grandmother's jewelled spitoon – it's your colonial legacy son.

(Pause.)

My beautiful brown boy, my sweet son, welcome to your world.

The Photograph (Part Two)

Picture of Sheku in a kilt appears.

SECOND: You are the only black man.

Ach!

But you are not that –

not today.

I imagine your children are all around you –

she is smiling at you over the top of their heads.

It's a heart-full day.

You pick up your son and you, smell the top of his baby head.

Kiss him and hold him tight –

a bit too long –

put him down when he wriggles –

crouch down to his level –

his eyes are pools drawing you in.

There are calls for you to join the lads but you linger

for a moment – with your son.

Family.

Fix his shirt which has become untucked.

She places a hand on your shoulder.

You put your hand on top of hers.

It's a heart-full day.

AAMER ANWAR'S OFFICE

FIRST: I sit in his office in Carlton place. Sit amongst the folders and folders and he looks out at me from his mountain top of papers, threatening to topple, topple something

…He says –

THIRD: *(Aamer, is ready – indicates for her to begin)*

– Right, okay.

FIRST: And then he is distracted by laptop ping and phone buzz *(Aamer picks up his phone)* and my questions have turned to vapours and have left me as he turns back his attention to me, I pick up the threads and try to weave something, to ask him something, that question, that will help me make sense of this, ask something, get something that will make sense of it all for me. And as he talks and I take notes which fall away to the margins on my page…It's senseless, senseless – fuck! *(Pause.)* I'm aware I have taken his time and I've nothing but my own useless heartbreak and I'm no avenging angel. I'm no justice for you. I'm just a voice saying your name, asking others to say it too. Sheku. Sheku. Sheku. *(Pause.)* Putting down the facts I can hold, that I am able to carry, that I will be able to lay out. And it hurts. *(Directs her question to Aamer.)* What can art do?

THIRD: *(Aamer takes a moment to think.)*
I think it can be a start…

FIRST: *(Turns to audience.)*
Better I let him talk.

THIRD: *(Aamer looks out intently as if at a press conference.)*
"There has been an attempt to criminalise Sheku Bayoh in his death – the dead can't answer back but his family have answered for him. He wasn't 6ft plus, he was 5ft 10in. He wasn't super-sized, he was 12 stone 10 pounds. He wasn't brandishing a knife at a police officer. He didn't stab a police officer. In fact he wasn't carrying a knife when the police officers attended. PC Nicole Short talks of the fear of a murder taking place. The reality is that there was only one person that day who died – Sheku Bayoh. He was the only person whose body was covered from top to bottom in bruises, cuts and lacerations. He didn't attempt to stab anyone. He wasn't found with a knife on him. These are the actual facts."

Lament (Part Seven)

SECOND: Safe space they had said.

(Pause.)

Safe space they had said –

FIRST: like it was a given.

THIRD: Given.

SECOND: Like it was safe to be –

THIRD: – all of your choices.

FIRST: The good of you.

SECOND: The bad of you.

THIRD: The ugly – like all of you –

FIRST: – would be free here.

SECOND: That we would judge you –

THIRD: – as we judged ourselves.

SECOND: Holding space, a door held open, safe space they had said but that space so easily dissolves, like sugar boiled, our hurt floods through the air vents, rises up from shelves lined with good intent – and entitled anthologies titled – Hear me. Please, hear us.

FIRST: Patchy. Patches worn like the way my skin is browner there, lighter there, like sun dapples. Negligible in whispers, looks given to us like apology, hiding their eyebrows raised, eyes rolled exchanges, as they let us into space left in corners, in rooms that once stored boxes.

THIRD: And she finds me there declares herself an ally, like I am to congratulate her. Mistakes me taking the knee as worship, as gratitude, not defiance. Not power. Offers me her voice and replaces mine. Gives me helping hand, and I think to bite it, but I am full. Fucking full of it.

FIRST: They are screaming it's satire from the front pages, his face pink, hair cut like Trump. As if I wouldn't recognise the handshake secret there. The dog whistle, remember? My funny tinge? Remember? Half of me is trained to hear it.

THIRD: That I know that welcome. That the belonging, is conditional – only skin deep.

SECOND: Safe here in this place, this safe place, and we say, to our wayward sons, our daft lads – the lads!

THIRD: Come on pal, take it easy son.

FIRST: What've you taken son? What you on son?

SECOND: You cannae be out here, off you face son –

FIRST: – but they saw –

THIRD: Black man said black man, they saw terrorist said terrorist.

FIRST: Sorted it, in thirty seconds, over in five minutes. See it. Say it. Sorted

SECOND: And we said safe place, safe place, aye?

THIRD: But it so quickly turns bitter. Hostile. Shifts.

It shifts. Spinning. Spinning the wheel of fortune to shut door.

Our Welcome, that belonging on condition. This is a safe place – we said –

like it was a given. Generously Given. Like it was safe to be all of your choices.

The good of you. The bad of you. The ugly, like all of you would be free here.

That we would judge you as we judged ourselves.

Hear it!

Fuck!

Step out here into this hard bleeding ground. Look at all these cooling coals raked

with our bloody hands. Take these broken stories. These broken lives and lay them down, here and weep wi me. Rage wi me. His body make the last body, we turn into mythical monster, to be slain, hold him. Hold him. Hold those who loved him. Quiten yourself down now.

SECOND: Quieten yourself down now and listen – listen – just *(Pause.)*

FIRST: Listen to us, raking at coals to start a fire to spark a flame, to burn this *(Pause.)* burn this fucking house down.

THIRD: No! Stop! Do nothing. Do nothing. Let it burn… Let it all fucking burn.

The Photograph (Part Three)

Picture of Sheku in a kilt appears.

SECOND: And it was an empty space
    that you were yet to fill.
    It was waiting for you.

    The kilt still in the hire shop.
    Her dress still hanging up.
    Your children not yet scrubbed clean for the occasion.

    It was an empty space
    that you were yet to fill.

    And it is an empty space
    that you will not fill.

    An emptiness
    in the bedtime story, bath time routine, at the first day and all
    the firsts.

    That photie, that moment, now an insistence, that once –
    you belonged.

Thirty Seconds (Part One)

FIRST: Sheku Bayoh

THIRD: 29

FIRST: What strikes me from the evidence of the officers is that they approach the scene with the intention of using force.

THIRD: 26
    25
    24

SECOND: He's not running away, he's not, at that moment in time, creating a danger to anyone

THIRD: 23

FIRST: Two officers believed they were facing a terrorist incident
    21

SECOND: We lost a brother through the hands of the police.

FIRST: 19

THIRD: 18

FIRST: His muscles were bulging.

THIRD: 16

FIRST: He was not super-sized.

THIRD: 14
    13

SECOND: He would still be here, if he hadn't met the police that night…

THIRD: 11

FIRST: His two boys are struggling –

THIRD: 9
    8

SECOND: His was the only body covered in bruises and lacerations

THIRD: 6

    5

    4

FIRST: He was the only one left dead

THIRD: 2

FIRST: His mother is going through such pain. She is crying every day – her only son is gone. 'It's really hard for her, for us, his sisters, and the rest of Sheku's family. If Sheku did not come into contact with police he would be alive today.'

THIRD: 0

SECOND: I heard him screaming. It sent chills through me. I heard the man shout to get the police off him. They never moved.

Lament (Part Eight)

THIRD: The black cab driver does racist things.

The kids on the street are doing racist things.

The drunk men on the train do racist things.

My son's teacher does racist things.

My colleague does racist things.

My neighbours are doing racist things.

My politicians are doing racist things.

My prime minister is doing racist things.

My police are doing racist things.

My friends are doing racist things.

My family are doing racist things.

My lover is doing racist things.

FIRST: I am tired.

I am waking up

in harr days, the fog so thick, it slips under the mat, under my door, into my home

comes to me at the bathroom mirror, where I stand looking for myself

and seeing nothing of myself there. I walk out of my home –

increasingly at odds with myself here, and I am tired. I am tired.

SECOND: In the dreich.

I am head down.

I walk hurriedly past old dangers and into new – headlong into new walls –

trip into recently dug ditches and trench. Fall

into new cracks opened up by your heavy boots.

THIRD: I am stripped to the bone

in all your acid words –

in all your acid looks.

FIRST: My beautiful brown boy.
My sweet son –
welcome to your world.

Photograph (Part Four)

Ae Fond Kiss by Robert Burns sung by the women.

Ae fond kiss, and then we sever;
Ae fareweel, and then forever!
Deep in heart-wrung tears
I'll pledge thee, Warring sighs
and groans I'll wage thee.
Who shall say that Fortune grieves him,
While the star of hope she leaves him?
Me, nae cheerfu' twinkle lights me;
Dark despair around benights me.
I'll ne'er blame my partial fancy,
Naething could resist my Nancy;
But to see her was to love her;
Love but her, and love forever.
Had we never lov'd sae kindly,
Had we never lov'd sae blindly,
Never met – or never parted –
We had ne'er been broken-hearted.
Fare thee weel, thou first and fairest!
Fare thee weel, thou best and dearest!
Thine be ilka joy and treasure,
Peace. enjoyment, love, and pleasure!
Ae fond kiss, and then we sever;
Ae fareweel, alas, forever!

Lament (Part Nine)

THIRD: I read this article about the migration of eels. Och! I know – but there was this bit it said – something like – when the eels reach European shores they turn to glass. Ach!

It was in the newspaper – right beside stories of migrants drowning in the med – all those sons – daughters – mothers – fathers – brothers and sisters – like the eels – okay? All those men and women and children *(Pause.)* turned into something so easily missed. Like glass and you know glass? It can so easily break. It's so right – we change here – or no – no that – we don't change – but we become something other than who we really are – not to us but to – well – to them.

FIRST: She says – I wouldn't want to be a black man. She says –

SECOND: – I think about my nephews.

FIRST: I think about my son – I say. We talk in whispers. A white man asks if the empty seat is free. We say –

SECOND: – yes

FIRST: – and then bunch up to the very edge of the table – lower our voices once more.

SECOND: I remember hearing about it on the news.

FIRST: Yes I say. I think – I first became aware of it. Och! Maybe when something about the campaign came up on my timeline.

SECOND: What did you do then?

FIRST: – She says…Nothing – I say. Maybe I liked it – not liked – an angry face thing – shared it. I look down and I am tearful, suddenly, it surprises me, she says –

SECOND: – I know it's painful.

FIRST: Yes, it hurts. The man beside us is talking loudly at the waitress. We are silent until he settles.

SECOND: I was at the doctor's the other day –

FIRST: she says –

SECOND: – a locum.

FIRST: I know where this is going but I don't interrupt and then it's me and a – I remember at School – and then her –

SECOND: – I was on a bus the other day –

FIRST: – Me. I was in a taxi the other day – her –

SECOND: – I was on the street. –

FIRST: – Me at work, and we talk the whole time in whispers – huddled together. And then she says –

SECOND: – I am so fucking angry sometimes it just – slips.

FIRST: Me too I say. We order cake to share. Funny thing is, we only just met –

SECOND: Sorry

FIRST: – she said –

SECOND: – but is this seat free?

FIRST: Of course, I said.

SECOND: What is that you are reading?

FIRST: She said. It's this story. It was in the news, Sheku Bayoh –

SECOND: Yes – *(Whispers.)* you know

FIRST: – she whispers

SECOND: *(Whispers.)* I would hate to be a black man.

FIRST: Yes, I said.

SECOND: I think about my nephews –

FIRST: – She said. I think about my son – I said.

(Whispers.)

THIRD: My father loved to walk. He would walk so fast, I would struggle to keep up. We would leave my Nan's, walk down through Muirhouse toward to Newhaven, to the Walk of Leith, he would walk so fast, I would be, almost jogging keeping up wi him. He knew the city, he would say, like the back of his hand. Just before he died, I asked him why he always walked so fast. Och! To out run the … Oh I don't know … I just walk fast.

At his funeral, we had a piper and we all sang – *Should auld acquaintance be forgot*
And never brought to mind? We talked and talked about his love for Scotland. She had booked his wake in this working man's club, they all love him there, she said. He is in the domino club, she said. We all walked in after, aunties and aunties, my sister carried in this pot of Dad's favourite curry.

The men were all gathered at the bar, all staring at us. All in silence. We were ushered to the back room. As we laughed, and cried… Och! They… They turned up the telly.

FIRST: Sheku, I watched this documentary about what happened to you, after I went to my son's room. He was sleeping. His wee body laid out. I stood at the crack of light that came in from the hall and watched him. I listened to him breathing. I thought of your mother, of that photo from the documentary. That one of the two of you. You are both smiling at the camera but her smile is for you, right? It's because of you – I smile like that too – at my son – I smile at him – just like that.

2020

VOICE OVER: In November 2019, The Scottish Government confirmed a public enquiry will be held into the death of Sheku Bayoh after the Lord Advocate's announcement in 2018 that none of the police officers involved in Sheku's death will be prosecuted.

Justice Secretary Humza Yousaf has said that the statutory public inquiry will examine the circumstances leading up to the death of Mr Bayoh, the post incident management process and subsequent investigation into his death. The inquiry will also establish the extent to which Mr Bayoh's actual or perceived race played a part in events, if any. In addition, the inquiry will make recommendations to prevent deaths in similar circumstances.

SECOND: In 2020, a Scottish Government advert for a media manager to handle the hearing's press inquiries, says the inquiry "will be based in central Edinburgh and is expected to last around three to four years".

THIRD: Sheku's sister Kadi, forty-two, a nurse, in Edinburgh, said the predicted length of the inquiry had dismayed his family.

FIRST: 'We are heartbroken,' she said 'We have already waited five years and now it might be many more years. How long do we have to suffer? Why do we have to wait this long for answers? We have suffered enough. We have long given up hope that any of the police involved will be held accountable. We just want to know why Sheku ended up dying in such a brutal way.'

Thirty Seconds (Part Two)

SECOND: 1

2

3

4

5

6

7

8

9

10

11

12

13

14

15

16

17

18

19

20

21

22

23

24

25

26

27

28

29

30.

SECOND: A civilian witness told investigators, officers were lying across Mr Bayoh for several minutes.

THIRD: …a maximum of thirty seconds… appropriate, textbook stuff…

SECOND: Sheku's family say up to six of the nine of the officers were on top of him.

THIRD: He lost consciousness and never recovered.

The Final Lament

The final musical lament plays/is performed – to a backdrop of images of Sheku – the marches, protests and other images from the campaign – headlines and front pages of press coverage – press and campaign photographs of the family and Aamer Anwar. The street art of Sheku Bayoh and Black Lives Matter protests in Scotland with Sheku's name alongside George Floyd's.

THE END

Source Material

BBC Disclosure

Dead in Police Custody

https://www.bbc.co.uk/iplayer/episode/b0bw8f21/disclosure-series-1-3-dead-in-police-custody

BBC News

Sheku Bayoh custody death officer 'hates black people'

https://www.bbc.co.uk/news/uk-scotland-34529611

Inquest

Lord Advocate confirms decision not to bring charges against Police Scotland officers involved death of Sheku Bayoh

https://www.inquest.org.uk/sheku-bayoh-crown-review

Fife Courier

https://www.thecourier.co.uk/news/local/fife/259515/friends-and-family-of-sheku-bayoh-gather-to-pay-their-respects-in-kirkcaldy/

https://www.thecourier.co.uk/fp/news/local/fife/640551/police-officer-injured-in-arrest-of-sheku-bayoh-claims-bosses-refused-to-let-her-retire-early/

https://www.thecourier.co.uk/fp/news/local/fife/1018593/video-family-of-fife-man-sheku-bayoh-arrive-in-edinburgh-ahead-of-police-prosecution-decision/

https://www.thecourier.co.uk/news/local/fife/248264/sheku-bayoh-scottish-police-federation-and-family-lawyer-clash/

BBC News

https://www.bbc.co.uk/news/uk-scotland-50401339

https://www.bbc.co.uk/news/uk-scotland-46591551

https://www.bbc.co.uk/news/uk-scotland-46591551

Daily Record

https://www.dailyrecord.co.uk/news/politics/sheku-bayohs-death-blamed-drugs-22153927

https://www.dailyrecord.co.uk/news/scottish-news/sheku-bayoh-documentary-reveal-fresh-13746730

https://www.dailyrecord.co.uk/news/scottish-news/unseen-cctv-footage-sheku-bayoh-13747099

Al Jazeera

https://www.aljazeera.com/features/2019/05/03/sheku-bayoh-the-death-of-a-black-man-in-scottish-police-custody/

Guardian Newspaper

https://www.theguardian.com/uk-news/2015/oct/14/sheku-bayoh-death-in-custody-officer-violence-family-allege

https://www.theguardian.com/uk-news/2018/may/02/family-sheku-bayoh-sue-police-scotland-death-custody

Press and Journal

https://www.pressandjournal.co.uk/fp/news/scotland/1634566/bbc-show-raises-questions-on-case-of-man-who-died-in-police-custody/

PC Paton and PC Short – Scot Courts Docs

https://www.scotcourts.gov.uk/docs/default-source/cos-general-docs/pdf-docs-for-opinions/2019csoh35.pdf?sfvrsn=0

MH PRESS RELEASE

02/06/2015

DEATH OF MR SHEKU BAYOH – FAMILY LAWYER HEAVILY CRITICISED

(Issued on behalf of the Scottish Police Federation)

Glasgow, June 2, 2015: The legal adviser to the Scottish Police Federation has responded to criticism levelled at the organisation by Aamer Anwar, the lawyer representing the family of Sheku Bayoh.

Professor Peter Watson of PBW Law said: "The comments made by those representing the family of the deceased continue to promote a completely inaccurate and misleading account. The officer injured remains off work, has had several hospital visits and is now in rehabilitation. An examination by a leading Consultant confirms her injuries were significant. The injuries have been documented and photographed.

"The officers involved have never refused to provide statements. It was agreed at the outset with PIRC that they would revert to us when they wanted statements and when they were clear on the basis that statements were to be given. PIRC emailed me this morning at 10:46am asking for our assistance to organise interviews and we answered at 11:29am confirming we would be pleased to assist. Those are the facts."

Brian Docherty, Chairman of the Scottish Police Federation, said: "Mr Anwar can try to throw whatever mud he wishes but the fact remains that a petite female police officer was violently assaulted by a large male and believed she was going to die as a consequence. In directing increasingly hyperbolic, inaccurate and bizarre rhetoric at the Scottish Police Federation, one could be mistaken for believing that Mr Anwar being at the centre of attention appears to be of greater importance than allowing the investigation to proceed without interference."

ENDS

SHEKU: THE INJURIES

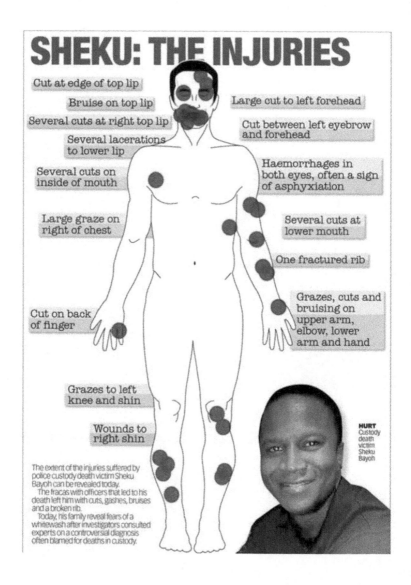

Cut at edge of top lip

Bruise on top lip

Large cut to left forehead

Several cuts at right top lip

Cut between left eyebrow and forehead

Several lacerations to lower lip

Several cuts on inside of mouth

Haemorrhages in both eyes, often a sign of asphyxiation

Large graze on right of chest

Several cuts at lower mouth

One fractured rib

Grazes, cuts and bruising on upper arm, elbow, lower arm and hand

Cut on back of finger

Grazes to left knee and shin

Wounds to right shin

The extent of the injuries suffered by police custody death victim Sheku Bayoh can be revealed today.
The fracas with officers that led to his death left him with cuts, gashes, bruises and a broken rib.
Today, his family reveal fears of a whitewash after investigators consulted experts on a controversial diagnosis often blamed for deaths in custody.

HURT Custody death victim Sheku Bayoh